This Book is Dedicated to
Mary Sinclair & Dr. Joshua Epstein

Also to
Stephan Caldwell & Will Elliott
for their endless support & friendship
for both myself and my husband

Mr. George Paul
who has been like a son to me
and
Nona Blundo
whose love has been
Unflinching.

Illustrations by
Richard E. Schiff
Life Member/Art Students League of New York
©2006 ALL RIGHTS RESERVED

ISBN 81-8253-066-0
Printed in India by Cyberwit.net

Mary Barnet

The
New American

Selected Poems

I Am Both Rich and Poor

I am both rich and poor,
Both happy and sad.
I am me, I am you ;
I am the changes of my life.

I have all and nothing ;
I possess the world.
I stand by your side
One, as on any Happy Birthday.

I dance with joy
Yet stumble lame ;
Happily onward I sing
Sometimes I am lost in the sadness of this world.

I hold the child of my flesh.
I am childless ;
I cherish my issue
As my voice touches this land.

I give you the shells I have gathered on the beach:
My hands cannot hold the sea :
My heart is full,
For life is mine.

Three Variations

I. Moment

I have always wondered
are these white blossoms of the cut Gladiola living ?
Is this
Spring dying ?
Are these dead flowers ?
Isn't it Spring somewhere always ?
What lives a moment
Is yet a part of life.

II. Gladiola

green stemmed Gladiolas
pistils protruding from the largest silk white bloom.
soft green leading up the stem to buds
which may or may not blossom
to give off the sweet smell
before the stem dies

.III. Infant

budding flowers
as white as the deliverer's white coat.
a trumpet for a New Year the world does not hear.
calling out from the womb of life
a bud like an infant whose cord has been cut
will sh. grow to bloom ?

Homeless Man

A slight unidentifiable man
appeared several times
near the end of the millennium.
As if to peel the skin
from the fruit,
He took off his sweaty shirt and socks :
removed piece by piece
of this world as it is.

The great, spinning machine
returned his garments
warm and clean.

Without explanation he donned them
remembering his birth. How odd!?

Thunder

Darkest night
Illuminated by thunder ;
Vision building to dawn
All cleared by the song of sparrows.

Ancient Dream

What hour is this
Passing me on wingéd foot
Waiting not a moment
For an "older woman?"
I shall join in the *ancient games*:
The poem reaches forces
unleashed by the gods of muse within ;
We know in our hearts
There is nothing more serious than a dream !
Unless it is a dream become reality !

River
Dedicated to "Dad" at his Memorial service

Among the people of the mountains
There is a saying,
"Sleep when you can,
Rest when you are weary,
The time comes to depart
Even from your home."
I thought of this
Watching the boats pass down the river,
Wondering which would come
To take me on my way.

As If

As if a thousand years
One second made,
God makes himself known to us,
That we may do as he has bade.
There is no reason life's glory will ever fade.
Sky streaked with purple,
Royal robes for sunset and sunrise,
Always our love will suffice,
& we shall live midst the blazing glory
Of our happiness-trodden glade.

Over

Over the mountains
The sunset hovers red
Red sun and crimson clouds
The sight condenses
To a moment of awe
Full of portent
Tomorrow the prediction
Of today's light
Fading to darkness
And night dressing at
The end of this glorious display
Crimson fades to black.

Silent Triumph

Nine Canadian Geese at first light
Swoop in through the low-lying fog
Onto the Glimmerglass surface of Manitou Lake.
A young chief softly propels his maiden
Over the smooth waters
In a canoe whose strength
Is in the pressure of the water
On the almost tissue-like bark
Of the canoe he has made.
They glide together through the dawn
Like the hawk and his mate who soar above
Watching with two-foot wings
One hundred feet over the ground
With eyes so keen
They can see the heart beating
In the tiny chest of the mouse they will devour.

Terns and swallows flit and dive
With blue-green wings around
His Princess with the dove-brown eyes.
Taken by him on a dawn like this
From her elderly mother's long house
Near the mouth of the river
So recently called "Hudson"
By those who came to live on it's banks
From across the Great Sea.
Beneath the earth on that hill
There is solid rock
And Indian Pond lies only a score of feet away
In a grove of elms, maples, and willows.

Now the mature male turtle has boldly climbed
Onto a tree stump near the shore of the lake
They canoe today
To sun himself on another glorious morning
Of another glorious day.

Photo: Mary Barnet 1995

Sermon

She found, as if by instinct,
The world she had dreamed of so long ago.
She felt not alone but rather full of peace.
The peace that one finds in a good word
And in a smile
The sermon she had come to hear was
Life itself.

Truth, Revealed

The Mightiest Judge stands before us
Vanquishing all foes, and breaching all barriers
In order to vindicate self and world.
The Creator revealed, the reason and the plan ---
        Eternal beauty born
           In the eyes of humankind.

Love All Purple And Pink

Golden sky
Trees all purple and pink
My heart has risen
Cannot sink.

My home is your arms
Pleasured in tight embrace
Every rainbow is lined
With a portrait of your face.

With you I ride the sky
Purple and pink
The multi-color light
That is tomorrow
Does not ever blink.

Bird gold & birds black
Sun blares; rains fall
My joy is in the quite ordinary
Glory of the crow's call.

The Little

white butterfly
dancing, gleaning, gleaming
over the shimmering of grasses
full of sun - air like glass
and the polyglot sound of birds
where the leaning tower of our days
is ready to tip
the cup of our souls
full of sun
yet the tower of our strength
holds firm
'til it shall disappear
though we never see it gone...

As published in RA (RecursiveAngel.com)

Girlish

Girlish the trees rise
All around me
Life reaching into the sky
Without the least question
Why green pops from every branch
Or stars push me naked into the welcome
Soft, firm, arms of grandmother earth
So that I sleep on the warm hills
A blooming world's wisdom
Touched with the song of eternal creation
Beneath this timeless, loving, sun.

Beams

The lighthouse beams
Showing all its teeth
Glimmering across the skin of our creation
Rocking this cradle of the sea
Back and forth
This rocky, rolling world
Where we are shining fish
That dance in these waters
Nothing more than bits of sun-bright
Betwixt the iridescent waves
Midst pebbles on this beach
Resting calm; Cros't by winds
Offering up ourselves
To make this song beautiful on the ears
Twinkling in the sky.

Almost Set Free

Your sneeze is a gibbon
In his big iron cage;
The elephant trumpets
When you blow your nose.
As you calculate your work
On your brand new computer,
I am wandering Bronx Zoo's trails
With mother and sisters
In shiny Easter clothes
Adjusting my patent leather shoes
And my just purchased bonnet
Beneath the fine Spring rain
With the African animals
Almost set free.

Waiting I mpatiently

Stuck impatiently
In you towers and your dungeons
Where your wrist-band
Leaves you like a bird

Banded, yet unable to fly

Slowly, Slowly the Wheel Turns

I can feel it
Nearing the plateau
No more struggle
This I know
We're nearly done
With this long slow climb
I can feel the wind
On the plain now
I know
Happiness is mine.

Subdivided by Love

The inconsistencies of consciousness
Finds us unclothed
In a universe whose caresses
Leave us cold and clammy.
In the errors of love
Lost in arms
Unconcerned with the needs
Of desire, and reality.
Unknown questions tugging at us
Where kindness is unreal
Rationalizations cut us
Words dice our love
Into a salad of unrealities;
We are empty and alone.
Swimming in the sadness of crowds.
Clowns dancing through worlds full with
Painful reckonings.

Dinner

Was it the skunk
Or the groundhog
Who ate the tomatoes
Or perhaps
Did they dine together?

Flock

A great flock of white birds
Above me whirled
With silver tongues
And beaks of pearl.
Pure knowledge is my dumbfoundment
Before the ever reigning glory
of the universe.
To see with eyes of sky
The fire that burns---
Knowledge of God
In the hearts of men,
Giving sight to those
Otherwise blind.

When death blossoms as the rose
Take one last look around
Let my words grow
Through the end of our days
Be ever nearer.
Let your fingers hold the winds---
When death blossoms as the rose!

Horizon

howling in the mind's eyes
mountainous rising, reaching
a sky whose equinevision
enlarges the earth
whose inhabitants are giants
whose foot-long fingers touch the clouds
living in the rolling hills, within the mind
tight, tense with fending off today
that arises skyscraper-like
from foggy yesterday
we like woods that ooze
and flow, with words that blaze and blow
sometimes cold, yet with living warmth
our worlds glow
a mist of green
a tiny slime upon this earth
bouncing ball in a greater league
galactic contest in which
wiser eyes
see us tangled in earth-wide throws

Question or Answer

What question is it?
Or which answer
Reveals itself in the wind?
Whistling past this house
Howling from out our windows,
Changing to quietly falling snow?

Artist

I like to sit and think
In the evening
When it is quiet ---
To make my typewriter go rat-a-tat-tat.
I imagine myself a central figure:
King-pin of the dream factory
Clarifying major questions
About the source of life itself,
Overcoming all obstacles to eternity.

I stand with gifts
Before the giant door.

Curled Toes

the winds in the trees
trail leaves like stones
racing with each wave
up and down the beach
a generation of living bones
a skeleton that walks
far beyond death's reach
so that reverend chipmunk
the flesh of each day saves
as the leaves wave
free yet never alone
in the worls
torrents of water and air, racing
about our toes, curled.

I Sit and Wait

For the dawn of the storm night.
I will canoe these lakes.
I am no one's
Child.
I am every woman
I am glad
I am alive
I have held the cup of death
Always cast it aside
I abandon abandonment.
I am reborn.
Each day renewed.
I am renewed. I am!
I am! I am!

Speechless

Hardly time to gasp for breath.
Lost in the cosmic silence,
Speechless before the night sky.
Struck dumb before the daylight,
Empty of words But full of sight.

Bang

The world begins
again
Extending in eternal rythem
Through the eye of Time
Reaching back
Threads itself over and over again
The root of forever
Recreating endlessly the tapestry

That is our lives
A great forest of now
A constant profusion of
Joyous growth
Existence bearing its own
consciousness
Like a light, a fire
Nourishing tomorrow
Keeping us always
warm.

The Crow

The crow always returns
To our window tree
I bless him;
He blesses me!

The Fruit

I am the fruit of winter
Born when the days
Are dark and cold
Wandering the tundra of existence
Past youth
Into the warmer hours
Of a good life
Here among friends
I look beyond unhappiness
Into the sound of Being Itself:
Life sings so sweetly
I strain to <u>hear it all</u>.

When

Your gaze meets mine
A smile blossoms
Multicolor, omnific, smiles blossom
Holding the pungent, pink and purple fruit
Nourishing in us
Growing to BE
The hours that are
The children of our love.

Safe

She found her one & only
Safe refuge --- she reached the
True point of her journey:
the squirrels ate voraciously
And a pair of squabs
Wandered among the
sparrows bathing in a tiny puddle
as Mary Barnet's Welcome Inn
Once the best sanctuary in the trees
Hangs idle --- in need of repair!
To be readied for its second summer!

"Juggler" by Richard Schiff Acrylic on Canvas
Original destroyed in Studio fire 1994

The Meaninglessness of Words

men speak these same words over and over again
universal day and universal night:
stars that die; lightening temporarily bright.
our lives and deaths
insignificant as all our breaths.
the planets and the countless stars
will disappear, as will each highway,
and all our cars.

the feeling of our summers and winters
is real.
hour to hour
our lives and love turn
we must build our own shelter
create a real world
reveal the darkness
as a clearing ,good and safe.
we must refuse to destroy
our love of life must find a home
in this first and only world.

we are dancing together now
arm in arm.
then, yielding to sleep,
we lay curled side by side.

The Darkness of Your Day

The rushing of the wind
Through the mind's eye, the sky
When light we cannot see
Comes and touches, such is
The darkness of your day
The un-sensing calm
Of the prest, the rest
Of numbed fear and the pre-stilled tear.

Untitled #4

It was one of those nights when the sailing
Is very clear and i knew i wanted to go
Below into the sea ; not calm but completely
Windless.

New Orleans

Untitled #5

this place
another world seen bare
from the road of so many worlds
among which i sit
and where i am
worldless.

New Orleans

Untitled #6

when we have seen the choice
it has already been made
spreading joyous or
alone in a hundred cities
i will ride this wave to the land
it promises to reach.

Mexico City

We Rose Trembling

We rose trembling thru your water
Emerged and saw the land green
Sparkling as wet seaweed
Spotted with roaming life
Barns on your chest
Soft red flesh flecked with with hooves
You cannot be mine
But through your forests
i smelled fresh grasses.

There are fields in Texas
Yellow like Van Gogh
There for a moment i thought i had found my home.

Texas

Breathing Regularly

Careful so as not to disturb the stillness of an extended
moment
Life was spreading out before me ;
A path through a garden
Tier on tier of experience
Tangled bushes from which roses emerge.
To look out on an even, gliding expanse of
Awareness above the sun-soaked lawn
Where each clump of somnolent grass envelopes
One mind in one thought :
The clean multiplicity of painless comprehension
Huge in its motionless extension.

An ocean of dew in a sparkling takes the eye
And loses it in the wonder of the sight.

Houston, Texas

As Night Descends

A distant fence squeaks in the wind
From across the border
A boat whistles into the wind
This is an evening lonely a childhood's
But the moments' enchantment is gone
For the deserted land I wander now
Stretches past friends and as night descends
Into a shudder.

The Sun Is Rising On Me

Alone in a bed
In Mexico City my illusion of security has disappeared.
There is only the light entering the tiny window -
Perhaps this is from a street lamp -
I close my eyes and it does not matter.

Awakening

Yesterday's tomorrow is today
As my roots strain to reach their source
I stretch toward the light
Freeing me to touch this world
Whose painful light
Is so beautiful
And so welcome.

Dream

What I have dreamed
Never to such a world as this could I convey
Much less than any man could lengthen this day
For though happily I myself to this life consign
Yet will I live as I may.

Though still on me life's cruelties prey
Life herself is my shrine.
To the source of All, I am but a face ;
This life will I live out,
Addressing each day with a little simple bravery,
Waiting to see tomorrow sprout
From yesterday's joys and sorrows
Into the hands of myself :
This day's devotee.

Stars Crashing

The sight of stars crashing
And the sound of planets whirling
Befuddle me.
All that I can see
Disappears before I can grasp it.

Yielding Up Tomorrow

We see our dreams made fruitful at last
Yielding up tomorrow ripe in our hands
As warm as sunbeams
We glean all we hope to be
At last we travel from our inner place
Traversing all the void into a glad world
As our secret abode expands
Into every day.

A Love Poem

Why have you left me?
I can no longer sing
     of what was my great joy.

If only I could have spoken
When it mattered...
     but that time is gone.

Once so long ago,
I glimpsed your hour
     standing by the roadside.

Thanksgiving

How I ever passed the eyes of time
To reach this ledge
Is a miracle of sustenance,
For hungrily searching I have found
The words that were made for me.
For though men usually wish for the best,
They see the worst in their commerce with the world.

Sighting the stars when the beauty of the world lies
before them,
Never seeing the light all around
When they can visit their own darkness
Day after day.

Untitiled #10

long ago
the words
"I am alone
in an empty universe,"
struck me upon the brow ;
since then,
struggling
sometimes sinking
always growing
above me
the many facets of a full sky.

Cup

I am full to the brim ;
I have drunk of life.
Now the thirst I wish to quench
Is for silence :
To quaff the calm waters
Beyond despair,
To hold an empty cup--
To be filled with the void.

Path

The details of our lives are trivial.
Winter is harsh ;
Summer always passes.
Like the wind our lives
Cut a golden path into the darkness.

Poem

Each of us creates what she can.
Perhaps my work is like the child
That died before he was a man ;
Never read and less commended,
Never greeted by those for whom it was intended.
Its life can never pass our seed,
Yet I think a poem, like a man, can bleed.

Song of the Mute Horseman

Always then I listened for
A voice from the darkness.
Now I hear
The wordless music of the spheres :
The sounds of time passing
As the years slip by ---
The song of the flute,
A tree falling in the forest
Or the unspoken words of the saxophone.
It is so varied...
It s all the same.
It is the tune of the mute horseman
Riding first toward us
But now away
At an ever increasing speed,
Disappearing into a misty horizon
Beneath the purple skies of a polluted sunset.

Forest

In this forest of light
Wandering with creatures in the night
The hungry beast in me
Stalks the singing bird I hold
Perched on the edge of eternity.

Wild Creature

The forest is a very good place
To learn how
To make a poem -
Free and simple,
Revealing with shining hand,
Out the womb of the soul
Our creativity delivered
As a wild creature's foal.

Small Things

I cannot tell you how
All my dreams are coming now
Small things are mine
And the wind
Before me in the trees seems to bow.

Early Afternoon

In my joy I am impervious to pain ;
I stand with wonder in the rain,
I am ready to walk a thousand miles,
To touch and feel and grow
Free of all restraint, while,
As the pristine showers end,
The clarity of this discovery ---
The beauty of this day ---
Astounds me !

Frogs and Crows

In our youth
We spoke of things that did not matter
We spoke of frogs and crows
And beasts that walk on tippy-toes.

When we remember the same words
We can be warm
In the cold reaches
Of the universe and on its windy beaches

Runner

In the philosophy of joy
I am a runner
Nearing that first full circle,
Passing the post,
Each moment closer
To the final wire.

Safe

She found her one & only
Safe refuge --- she reached the
True point of her journey:
the squirrels ate voraciously
And a pair of squabs
Wandered among the
sparrows bathing in a tiny puddle
as Mary Barnet's Welcome Inn
Once the best sanctuary in the trees
Hangs idle --- in need of repair!
To be readied for its second summer!

At Nine We Open the Door

I flip on the sewing machine switch at 7.
My husband has been up since 5.
In the Fall, customers with coats
Which must be dry-cleaned immediately (if not sooner!)
Pour in, leaving the dirt of their days
The spillage of their meals,
And some small portion of their earnings.

This is our store ---
We sacrifice for it.
Morning, like the nursing Mother Earth
Gives us both a few minutes of serenity.
My brother-in-law, a cop on the night shift in the South Bronx
Brings us tea and the most delicious corn muffins in Queens!
Sleep and meals are catch-as-catch-can:
No breaks here.
I cook at 11 PM, for myself, and hopefully my husband.

The boy who helps us brings us tea in the afternoon;
We are too busy; By six it's cold.
The milk in the tea is curdled
We must pour the remainder down the sink.
("We can afford another cupful,
Some can't," my husband points out.)

A murmur long unheard, within me now
Like a pure spring beneath a mile of stone
Wonders silently if I can afford to spend another year this way.
The thrust of my life has been dulled,
My pen all but stilled ---
My real thirst unassuaged.

Sonnet

When first I glimpsed you I was only two
Sister Peg and I were playing our spinning game.
Forty years later when we met I did not know your
name.
I could barely talk I felt so blue
But from one deep searching look of yours, I took my
cue.
I had heard no mention of your artistic fame
I myself was lost in past years' gathered pain.
In your eyes I saw all would be good and new.
I perceived a renewal of all possibility.
You grabbed my lifeless soul and gave me hope :
I felt love before me and in your eyes I saw it ---
Through this darkness I no longer grope
Now a great dark world is relit.
Discovering in you the glow of each day
My path joins yours as we walk together and together
lay.

The Hasidic Men

They are happy together---
Perhaps, thinking of the chanting
And the dancing they do to praise God.
But facing the world alone :
One Hasidim on his way for groceries
Is alone on a street of bantering South Americans.
He is something different, even hateful to them !
He knows this.
Whether it be the fear of pogroms or the Holocaust
Or a simpler, more general angst---
A loneliness for God and prayer
An outsider cannot know !

Gur Emir: King's Grave

I can only see Samarkland in a picture book
One of the great cities of Central Asia
Where ornate gold and lapis stucco decorate the
mosques and mausoleums
Great kings and thousands of slaves
Labored centuries to build.
A flourish of color in a mosaic faience
---like a tree that falls in the forest---
Unseen by western eyes.
Timur, a fierce conqueror
Builds himself a mausoleum with yellowish green onyx
tile on the walls waist-high.
The railing around the tomb is finest alabaster.
The slab covering the grave is one great piece of
nephrite jade.
One conqueror tries to lift it---it breaks in two ;
Then on the day Hitler invades Russia
The soviet archeologists lift the great Timerlane's
crumbling corpse from his grave.

A Jar of Words

I must pause
Survey the work I have done
In this season of menorah and crib beneath cross
Approaching the worldly new year
With what I have won.

Certainly I have not pierced the Veil
But I have fought some devils and won
Housed the little children within, whose wandering has
ceased.
I have grasped the lonely year :
A few tales have I spun.

The year brings nourishment
For the poet I have become :
An education of night terror's cries
Frees the lovely new year
Word by word, as if from a jar of letters, my craft finds
a course to run.

LOSING HANDS

"My husband and I own a tailor shop.
It's quiet today : I' ll sew these buttons and tell you
about my sister.

She is a baby doctor
in the noisy emergency room of Children' s Hospital
of Philadelphia.
Some of her patients and their parents call her,
'whitey doctor.'

Here, let me catch this hem ..."
"today two sisters came in with knife wounds,
gang warriors whose parents must accept their
children's fates ;
they were very close, the mother said ;
one I sewed up ; the other died.
I was relieved I didn' t have to tell the dead girl' s sister.
I feel a responsibility
I call my patients' parents on my day off ;
they are rarities - small time winners
with a losing hand.
Often my white coat is covered with blood."

Och ! I' ve pricked my finger ; but let me go on,
blood flows freely on our streets,
the doctor' s fatigue lights the death of the flower,
civilization ;
here all virtue that buds : black, white, brown, and
yellow
is obscured by the pretty colors of the blossoms
with which we mark the milestones of our lives
as we pass the homeless and the beggars by.

My husband and I work as one in a busy shop,
There is peace, but, but elsewhere : no."

"midst the clatter of death
there is another reality, and
there are those who do their job
others who really care.
most of the people trapped in the barrio are too bitter to
care ;
most people don't want to see the children, abused and
neglected
Crack babies and those with AIDS
This is the collapse of our common humanity-
there is a war going on in our cities"

    "all around is the devastation
    we try to hide from what really touches us all-
    we cannot long escape !"

Gathering

We gather in the garden of our childhood
Stone walls scattered
Basking in the sun.
All walls
Crumbling
Beneath a new rain.

Glad sun showers
Where hours
Like the boulders of old walls
Are arranged in the shapes of our love.

South Jersey Lover

A North Jersey girl of fifteen
Her Finches could not keep captive.
They flew about her room.
In Spring, through an open window,
They flew away ;
She feared they'd freeze though free
When Winter came.
She did not know
What beyond her window lay.
She forgot those birds for thirty years
Til she herself learned
Home's worth that day
Such Finches perched on the windowsill
Of the cozy home
She and her South Jersey lover have made.

41

All Logic Cannot Quiver

All logic cannot
Justify the end of life.
End is but a word, a creation.
Always is the more of time : forming men with a finite
spark

To ponder
the wide loving, girth of hours
ride this collective rollercoaster yet, comprehend only
in flashes

knowing but the reach of existence
And doubting the truth of forever
Which squirms
Beneath the All of Time

Pausing, beginning again, quite real
Incomprehensible
The unborn that forms

Tomorrow, already glowing.
The touch of Cannot be Known
Quivers awake

Out the revered darkness
the glorious surprise of light :
Rebirth, slumber

The stupefying imperfection
Of words and our vision
For a God without eyes

Excepting in we
in whose wanderings of Being
Is understood Only

In darkness that bears light
In sleep that rises again
and again, yet cannot know
Something so huge as all.

So we rise and smell flowers
Pink and blue --- the sunset
Oh ! the glorious fortune of life !

Unseen Circus

At the unseem circus
Eternal life is the door-prize
The invisible clown saves us all
Everyone ! Laugh at disaster !
The booby prize is love.

We all get certificates of Normality
Which Emmet Kelly wears in his hat.
The acrobats dance in the air :
We all continue until the Highwire collapses
And we adjourn until tomorrow.
Again the elephants walk !
Another night, until they are ready to sleep.

"Circus"" by Richard Schiff Acrylic on Wood 1991

Forever

after our kiss the moment extends
forever in never-ending line
the trees of my homeland america
like the cypress of france and spain
reach out on the horizon
into the mellow golden
yellow lake of receding afternoon
pines gathering for worship
and the rippling waters
of the lake of the Great Spirit
where the island of the turtle -*tulipitmenipit*
sits like a maiden
upon the waters of our grandmother
the whirling dancer
that is our earth.

The Sun Rising

Like a lump of soft yellow butter
On my toast, waiting to be spread
I devour this day
Experience crisp and sweet
The slight taste of salt
Tantalizing my mouth and nostrils
The jelly reaches my tongue
My brain is alive
With the always newness of Time
Reaching to a shout
The full taste of each hour puckering
Washed down with fresh juice---
The fruit of this bright world !

Forest of Pure Light

No longer running away from the bright rays of the sun
Remembering only the honor of those who stand strong
and firm
Before the sometimes brutal and ugly trials that are a
part of some of our lives

Each day we abandon yesterday
We give ourselves to the creation of each squeaky-clean
new morning
With the rights and honors good only can ultimately
achieve for us
We stand together now in the beauty of our real
humanity
In the ultimate joy
Of the worlds we have found, and
Each minute, hour, day, and year
Stretching before us
In pristine splendor - A forest of pure light

Fourth Of July

My elderly mother
reminisces about the Civil War cannon.
"What happened to it?" she asks, quite innocently.

She remembers the Civil War veterans
on canes, missing legs, arms
who came every Fourth of July
to ring the great bell that stands nearby.

The cannon is gone; the park filled with
alcoholics and addicts.
She imagines one blast of that cannon,

turned to face these "trespassers" on her park
would awaken the citizenry and clear the park
so an old lady could go out and sit.

Personal Homeland

On a Friday
After the end of work
The terns and swallows
Are flying through the garden
And over the house,
The doorway lined with roses
Red, and pink, all a'bloom
When the pond by the barn
Full and green with algae
Is a delicious drink for the sparrows.
Soon the raccoon nesting in the towering Spruce nearby

The 'possums and groundhogs from their burrows
emerge
At sunset, the wild rabbits are done eluding the hawks,
But what catches my ear with a sweet childhood
memory
Is the passing of the Ice Cream Man in his truck
With this repetitive chimed melody:
The old standard,
Turkey in the Straw,
Echoing down the years, and
Along the streets bordering this, my homeland.

Winter's Pause In the Sunlight

This is the sacred moment
When a red pavilion bird-house hangs
Gently swinging in our cove
In the afternoon winter sun I sit bundled,
Huddled against the rising wind
In anticipation of a warm morning breeze:
Joyous at the approach of Spring!

Growing Up

Up unfamiliar stairs that morning
A small woman climbing still half in sleep
Lost in delusions of youth
Beholding: a storm cloud licking the ceiling;
A pall of smoke that prepared the meal
Of heat, of wood cracking, burning, scaling.
Flames growing and growling behind the walls -
She floundered in hopes of dousing this gruesome fact
In favor of the promise that was this day.
Too much seen she must carry the tale
Down stairs to lead soon...nowhere.
Blissful shower ended, her lover hears the alarm:
"There's smoke upstairs, I think!"
(Not yet daring certainty!)
Quickly! Quickly! Up the stairs!
Speedily spreading, red; the swollen, furious infection
Over their heads flames burst above the bed
(They thanked God after
They rose early), but the fire-
Extinguisher could not heal
His burns as from across the yard she stood
He stood, surrounded by fire
And firemen. While the flames ate up the air
He watched his dreams extinguished.
Angry flames gobbled his world
Raging - Undisciplined - Cackling!!!

The order of his home a shamble of cinders
Grabbing up all the art of his days
- The love in his life's saved memories -
All things great and small flung as dust of nothing

To the farthest corners of nowhere.
They saved a few things
She dragged them in his daze of loss
He hauled them in their terror
To a tiny house from this shell.
Nearby. A m an and woman waited, and watched
Above blue flame-clear fields
Seasoned beams strong as tempered steel raised
A house wed by amber grew cool and hard.
Christmas Eve they returned
Their home new
Still the fear of walls would not subside
In years, they might sleep again
As earlier, in older years
In the peace,
The gift of disasters, Overcome.

Between

I am lost in a land
Somewher e between
Joy and sorrow.
Once again I ride into your world
As if it were the new Jerusalem.
I --- hungry for sleep
Yet hungering a little more for life.

With Gratitude To Sylvia Plath

Killer bees attack
Like a squadron
Presaging conflagration
These warriors show no mercy!
Buzzing. buzzing, buzzing...
These hum their oft deadly tune.
Woman on the porch, disaster looms:
Terrible Hoards threaten to descend.
Gath'ring about the ice cream she is churning,
Fire-like - Nature's anger travels...
Terror! Midst the swarm!
Cannot be stopped, are not stationary like thorns.
The arrival of the drones
A thousand stings!
Screams! As the swarm surrounds.
Remember! Yellow! Ora nge! Murderer!
"Herr God, Herr Lucifer
Beware,
Beware"
Beware!

Happy Birthday Engagement From "My Kids"

Husband, your little niece
In search of cash for charming Christmas gifts
And having a new beau
Tried in vain to sell the "slightly used" engagement ring
She bore into our home.

"They said they'd take it back, but they won't!
The quality is not as good as I thought!"
she gasped in youthful frustration.
"Nelson really ought to have an electric can opener for
Christmas---
(He was her extremely muscular young brother!)
I really need to get something nice for all my brothers
and sisters!"

Childless, Richie and I looked down at the table
tenderly thinking
I ventured--- "My Birthday is in two weeks...perhaps..."
"Will you take a hundred? Is that good?
I can't give it to you until next week when I get my
check."
"Oh yes, Thank you, Uncle Richie,
I can always count on you"

Thusly, I had my "O'Henry" Birthday gift.

Cruel Ruffian

Wisdom that comes from struggle
Farm Hand, nothing of his own
Not even himself

Nails a wire to the side of the barn;
Attaching it to a broom handle
He slides a broken glass bottle-neck over the wire,
Plays his home-made bass
And wails to the wailing wall of that
Slave-owner's barn
Content in the music of his soul.

We "free" him with nothing but the
Clothes on his scarred back;
House him in slums a hundred years more;
Work him near starvation in field & factory;
Burn him on crosses,
And shoot him down at his door.

Who is the cruel ruffian?

Our Kingdom of Heaven

Forfeit the Kingdom of Heaven
For me. Be my lover.
I will have no other god before you
You will have no other, but me.
<u>This</u> is the land of our forgetfulness
When life seems much more
Than a pause between sleeps.

The Light Appears...

The light appears on the mountains:
Joy is mine --- I only ask
The freedom to make myself
As I am wanting to be.

The Golden Delight

That releases me
From everyday care;
The joy that is
mine, the peace---
The whole of sky
Where I find myself
Lost in eternity.
The moment enveloped
That hour caressing my neck:
The animal - the ape -
The jewels of this earth
Before, behind
All about.

me, the sounds of life
singing on the wires
Telephone gone wild with deals.
Cash for the supermarket
Rent for the landlord---
Perhaps a vacation (oh!
for a vacation I would give
Some fine portion of my
Kingdom
That rings with Telephone
And Fax and Cable Network
Computer (Audio and Video
A contest for which
perhaps the prize
Is the world!

All Around
As we talk with the night

In the sunshine
We discuss.
Sunrise and the sunset appear.
We appear;
We disappear.
We sleep longer than we wake,
Perhaps never to rise again.
Perhaps always racing;
Treading the darkness like water,
Silvery and soft on our dreams;
Shimmering as we talk
With the night.

Un-natural father

In the hours that pass
and the minutes-
I see one face turning away
And a thousand more turning
To face me;

There is no end
But the end of Time.
We stretch to see
The march of eternity beyond the cradle
And the grave,
Into the bright Sun-Time of bursting
Universal womb that gives us Today
Wrapped in memory and presage
Of Time like a great wave reaching Far Beyond,...

The Cicadas are Buzzing

The room is dark and warm.
The moon lights the woods.
Nearby,
Dark beaches await the dawn.

Perhaps,

Tomorrow will drape herself like a cloak over our pain
In anticipation of the bursting flower
That is now
The warm blood we drink as our nourishment
Milk of mother and lover
Rose red
Yet pure as clouds over a land
Unbesmerched by man's corrosive hands
That feed and befoul
And do not know any contentment with today.

Our nourishment is
Not meat, but clouds;
The air about the grasses that blow.
The very wind is my home.
Since I have found my home
I am here, always!
Dwelling in the joy
Of my own creation
Free to find happiness in a land that extends
Beyond all mortality
Into the universal reality of my existence,
My arrival into the world of fondest imaginings
All love made real!

Working Late

The newly pressed shirts
Stand like silent sentinels
As first light nears
We step into the city streets
Locking the cast iron gates behind us.
Now the store is silent, too.
The lampposts light the trees
On our short walk home.
After dawn showers
We go to sleep at last.

Passion & Pen

The passion of our youth is spent:
The beauty that once blossomed
on our firm bodies has faded;
your hair is sprinkled with gray.
We have lost the rage we once cradled.

I wish I could give you more---
I am like the fisherman lost in the storm
Who, after the winds have calmed,
Finds she has neither pole nor line

But only her eyes, and her arms,
And her pen.

Endless Panorama

Over lake after lake
The panorama of beauty is endless.
But I am caught in nothingness
While life whirls all about.
At last I see my world
Reaching for me.
I find peace
In the reality of joy.
Life is mine;
I am the land, and the water.
I am real, singing
A continuous hymn to Creation;
Hurtling in my awakening
Past crowds of pine
In my small canoe.
The dragonflies twitter
In waves of heat.
Flat green leaf-pads
Drape themselves over the water beneath the sun:
Water lilies gather
To celebrate the birth of light.

The Golden Triumph

The golden skies in triumph
Acquiesce to day's demise;
Green reflections turn to blue.
Blue skies are purple in dying hue.
Beasts, great and small,
To sleeping places creep and crawl.
But some creatures rise: play in darkness.
The 'coon dances
The wolf does bay.
'Neath the earth in tunnels everywhere
Beneficiaries of death, beetles and worms
(Beware!) do play.
Quiet whirrs and dances;
Life takes her own chances. But ah!
Dawn now nears
Cleansing all her fears.
Booming silence in light resounds!
The sun in Spring
Upon the planet pounds.
Trumpeting infant birds in new-born down
Gift humankind his living crown.

Less Directly

The sun was just right.
Through the dusty window it caught the light.
Off the top of my fruit juice can it flashed.
As I directed it, upon your soft brown hair it splashed.
"Who is this woman?" looking at me, you thought.
I was glad with what I had wrought.
Playing like a child,
I turned my head and we smiled.
Must this hour too pass?
There, it's happened, the sun's slipped into a crevasse.
This sun shines less directly.
And I have spoken incorrectly.
I had not the courage to shine this light on you.
As you finish your meal, I finish mine too.
I think of all the hellos never said
Wondering how time might have confounded,
What hours we might have invented
Might from this hour now be descended?

Suddenly (I Cannot See)

The pigeons are gathered in the park
pecking at the bread crumbs the old woman has left
them.
Then, quite suddenly,
disturbed by something I cannot see
they disappear in flight.

Passing

Tomorrow
Now is given us
So that as children after we grow and change
As adults we malinger and fuss,
In old-age curse and cuss this fate.

Ranging from waterhole to waterhole we find ourselves
Nearer always to the source of passing time.
Our trav'ling does not abate until
Dusk seals this note;
In darkness or by moon-light
We are one with the now
Eternal passing of the night.

Tales

Brave up to the storm
All is too soon ended
We are left with our deeds
The memory of the faces we saw
And a few fond tales.

Occupant

The brown-spotted bananas are there
In the bowl with the apples your Aunt brought us
And the pears I bought to bait the traps
For the mouse living under the sink in our kitchen.
I am wondering
If the three mice
Who have given their lives in our year here
Were mother and son
And grandson
Or merely occupants of the same apartment ?

Day into Night

Now the long shadow of sunset disappears;
Imperceptibly, day slips into night.

We step with reverence into the darkness.
The stars tremble above us.
The wind in the pines is moaning.
Like a wildfire,
Drunk in its magnificence,
Life whirls by.

One Short Week

One short week ago
I sat on the beach;
The darkness shimmered off the water.
Cold waves caught you
As you played in the sand.
I perched on the hill
trying to keep warm -
You were damp
And we were wed.
I thought to myself,
"Surely, this is material for a poem."
I knew I would write later
But the significances are lost in that time.

I sit in the dark courtyard
Behind our workplace.
You are asleep,
Weary of the day's toil,
Resting before a good night's work.

As always, I am writing in the darkness
By your side.

Old Sinclair Grandmother

The Roosters are crowing through the night streets of this City
Beside them, perched in trees, my Old Mom saw a white duck
Coming towards her, down the street in the snow.
[The rooster crowns old Sinclair's family Crest.]
Meanwhile, The Jazzman reproduction
Is the Christmas gift for dog-walker Frank
Good helper for Old Mary
He shoveled snow for her that 86th year
Would we could always have Christmas thus.

But now the little woods are cut down.
Perhaps the Hassidic girls
Will play next to their school.

The Summer Circus

Cardinals go shooting, crimson across the garden
Like saintly creatures shot from cannons;
All about, snapdragons are blooming
Burnt orange, high in Acanthus trees,
Swinging trapeze artists for a hot summer celebration.

Sorrow Danced Across Her Face

The sun could not penetrate his inner place:
Sorrow danced across her face.
Tears came,
He asked her to stop;
In the litany of love
Last love gone.
Pink flamingo rising into the skies
Above the deserted beach
Whose shoreline I wander now.
My response to his flight,
A prayer:
"Lord, fill my empty heart.
Perhaps I am free only in Your arms."
Tied here to the memory of early lovers
Until a chain reaction occurs:
Discovered; All thrown from this slave ship---
Chained at the bottom of a murky sea.
Some shall not rise upon the beclouded steps:
We will all escape mortal slavery….

Core

I am empty
In what should be the
Swirling cosmic inner core
A void-- a hollow cavern of touch
A heart that cannot be filled

But like damaged glass
Leaks out its life juices
Unable to experience
Always yearning
For love, self-satisfaction
Completion.

Warmth

in the depths of darkness
In the deepest hour of the storm
As snow falls all around
We cannot be touched by the cold.

A Thousand

Without light
There is darkness.
Somewhere lost in mist
There is a direction;
A thousand travel
A thousand different roads
Leading-- all of them--
To this same ending.

This Minute Today

My time
Is not an hour tomorrow;
It is this minute today.
I cannot stop.
Much remains to be done:
What I dreamed
Must now be seen whole.
To create,
To make something lasting,
To build with these hands,
This is the meaning
And the task this moment bestows.

Sun

I wanted to touch the stars
But I needed time away.
Tomorrow I pray
Time will let me reach into the darkness
To pluck a sun
Like a newborn from the womb!

Cup

I am full to the brim;
I have drunk of life.
Now the thirst I wish to quench
Is for silence:
To quaff the calm waters
Beyond despair,
To hold an empty cup--
to be filled with the void.

Travel

I pause
By the roadside;
My travel seems endless.
Do we find a destination in the moment?
Or retreat into our anxiety
Simply moving our bags
From one terminal to the next?

Window

I saw the darkness opening
To gobble me up.
Once again
I was a child alone in the night.
In that dark, empty well,
In the musty, moist depths
I have found no bottom
As in the deepest place within me
There is no home
Only the coldest air-- the great black hole
Rushing in through a broken window of my mind

Release

Rest easy now
This world will all be yours in time.
Call up your strength.
Scale not another wall;
Wait quietly in the garden
For your keeper of all these years
To come and release you.

Path

The details of our lives are trivial.
Winter is harsh;
Summer always passes.
Like the wind our lives
Cut a golden path into the darkness.

Two Worlds Collide

I. LEMON-LESS CHRISTOFO

Columbus long searched the seas;
his sailors grumbled lemon-less,
challenged his authority
for fear they must return from whence they came or die.
The curlew came
the last birds of the fall migration crossed his prow;
the birds, blown somewhat off-course,
calmed the men
discoverers of an already discovered land.

What exactly Christofo proved
not already known elsewhere
is doubtful. The birds did not stop
'til on the next leg of their journey southward, they
paused
to gorge themselves on
crowberries, crowberries, crowberries !
until, at double their weight, their breasts dripped with
purple juices
and they were ready to resume their flight.

Columbus began the destruction of the Americas
that continues to this day.
Eskimo curlew, his aid in great crisis,
was last sighted in Barbados in 1963 -
thirty years ago the last Eskimo curlew migrated from
Alaska,
to the tip of South America and back...
about twice the distance of Christopher's first complete
journey.

Though gorged, still delicate the curlew were;

following nature's command
they flew without fear.

In the end the hunters came
desiring to slaughter them, with everything else
beautiful and self-reliant
(so small in flight, and yet so strong).
A mass of birds like soldiers in God's army,
who never claimed the sky or pampas
except in passing through each year.

II. CURLEW

I glean and glide.
At the first sign of winter in the Arctic
I gather my young,
All of us full of fat to burn on our flight.
I follow the air currents;
Soon we are a migration of plover and curlew
Heading for Tierra del Fuego.
I ride the air drafts...
Heat rising off the crops and fields,
The air cool above the wooded areas.
I stop for a snack, weary and hungry, in Labrador;
Gorged on delicious berries, I am ready for the open
Atlantic.
Next stop: the islands of the Caribbean
where sky and water meld
sparkling blue, green, turquoise.
Stopping to eat here, and then, further south
I pause midst the cattle of the Llanos in Argentina and
Columbia.
Later, in September and November
I feed on the bounty of termites and other insects

The Cerreado and the Pampas yield
and, of course, the crowberries!
With a fare fit for a world traveler and gourmet...
I eat while basking in the sun!

I glide on streams and rivers of air
until I must return northward.
Nature tells me to mate
And where to bear my young;
Within me lies the self-perpetuating joy of living in the
skies.

It is the return:
Running the gauntlet of the hunters
Which decimates our number.
With one great bang after another
The hunters claim our lives and our freedom.
Year after year, they are there with their great guns:
We who fly on fat are a tasty meal.
The hunters are finally curbed
But the plover will have to fly alone !
My time is past and my family gone to hunters all !

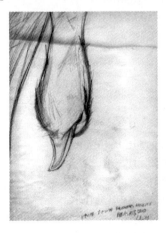

First Poem

The sun meets the air on a September day;
I yearn to jump up and fly - yet not away:
To feel as my soul - the trees;
As my mind I would know the wind.
But even with my sight so vast
I would still want a green fall leaf
And still a violet flower.
Would they would grow near my heart
And when it was threatened by storms of wind
And darkened by clouds
Then might even a tree conquer the wind
And show it the flower to play soft breezes upon;
So, too, by turning outwards once more,
To the form of one flower might I go.

And then could I,
with inknowing honest joy,
Turn to my love
caring no more to know
But only to see
And to be.

Poem

Each of us creates what she can.
Perhaps my work is like the child
That died before he was a man;
Never read and less commended,
Never greeted by those for whom it was intended.
Its life can never pass our seed,
Yet I think a poem, like a man, can bleed.

This Man Has Won The Bingo Game

Unexpectedly, six freshmen arrived
from the state university.
Unlike most days when she alone
Held a news roundup
Or led the wellest in exercise
Today became a Bingo game
For the residents of the Altenheim Infirmary.

"B-4," the smallest of the young men
Almost shouted to accommodate the deaf.
William 97 now but a policeman in his younger years
Told meekly of the stroke
That paralyzed most of his left side.
"Does anyone come to see you?" I asked.

"My wife's upstairs," he said, referring to the apartments.
"She's here because of me. She hates it here!"
"I-2," another youth shouted. "This will be
your last game. Clear your cards!"

William began to sob---tear dripped from his nose.
I looked over and saw a very old woman
Had smeared waste water over her face.

"B-2," another youth,
almost a boy announced to the large, full room.
"She's the best woman in the world I'm telling you,
She's the best in the world.
And it's all because of me.
All because of what happened to me!"

Seemingly from a distance
The boy behind the Bingo cage
Announced in a loud voice,"B-2, B-2"
Then suddenly the game was over
As a fellow at the far end of the dayroom called out.
"Bingo! Bingo! This man has won
This man has won!"

Sweet Time

Time:
Desert in flower;
You cannot hold her back.
She conquers that loss,
Reverses that curse,
And drowns the pain
Born in us.

I reach for you,
Sweet time,
Hold me close!

You can quell those devils
Dwelling yet
Within us.

Quiet Time

I cannot write a word
Or choose a rhyme.
But I listen
To my own quiet time.
I believe
In silence there is a song.

Night

Night envelopes me like a cocoon:
I am the caterpillar
only vaguely threatening to be a butterfly
hoping to hide the past -
to shroud it in mystery
like the man in the iron masque.
I am judge and judged in one long, tearful,
fearful trial.

Until I let the confrontation die.
make of my own flesh
the gown of the graduate:
student of the world,
in which I, self-crucified, rise again!

Returning on the Bus from Massachusetts

Another vacation over.
Another holiday gone..
Another bus to take.
Again I return alone.

Soon today will be
But a memory ;
This moment passes
So quickly into eternity.

Some say there is a plan.
I wait for some arrival.
Meanwhile I plot and plan
Another month of my survival.

I hope someday to pause,
Turn and see your face,
Stop and see the place
Where past and future interlace.

There are times
I cannot write or rhyme,
When this confrontation
Does not yield a line.

I wonder what it matters
That I sit alone.
Another hour passes.
I am returning home.

Where I Belong

I do not want to sing my sorrow;
You have heard it all before.
It is the song of silence I want to borrow
The quiet of a field covered by snow;
The tune the wind plays
Blowing up small hills from below.

When that sky is slate blue
All that exists is you
Walking along by my side,
Piercing me like this cold with your song,
Then drawing me out of this chill
Into your arms where I belong.

Quite a Storm

The warm days wane.
The cold, dark progression of time
Stains our lives with a gathering of tears--
In these eyes the frigid wind sears.
A constant storm passes before us.
The minutes fall like rain!

The Dry Cleaner's

Sitting among the racks of garments:
Men's suits, dresses, and dresses, and blouses and
shirts;
Gray, green, black, spotted and striped--
In the being of each I see lives
Which we, like practical theologians, must cleanse.

Daughters

I stand in this park named for Ole Bull
Brought here by the mad violinist's daughter
To dance without music
In a Pennsylvania forest with no electricity.
Instead the universal song of the woodsy creatures
Where large pine rise untouchable
Where our adolescent brothers laugh
At the earnest struggles of their little Sisters.
No song can compete with God's
Whose joyous laughter is eternal.
He is just and feels in his wisdom
The lessons
The perspective of our defeats.

Long Road

Far away the sky always stood
a god I could hardly see
Midst the smoke and smog.
Now above me I see the moon
A new world is looming
I want to see
Long before death
I shall be free
At last!

Passing on to You

Cleaning closets
I pass on what is mine
To you to wear & experience
The colors of my days
The worlds I have seen
Here for you
Now & then, again & again
You can travel through
'My worlds
I give them all to you. '

Remember

Dark green sea-pools
Eyes drawing me in
To their own realities
Swimming in tomorrow
In your vision
I am whole.
But when I am too small
I drown in your worlds ---
I was not taught to swim
Remember?

Ring

A ring of little pebbles
Shattered by a wave
Clattering one upon another
This is the music
Within us lays
Within our universe resounds
So that, in each of us
Resounds a new day.

Since You Are Gone

The groundhog walks
In light of day in our yard;
I notice every leaf:
How the Trees of Heaven sway.
My voice is quelled.
You cannot hear
What I might say---
Knowone knows
My love of what was our Everyday.

Only the solice of your embrace
Can revive my heart again.

The Flow That Is

Music of my creations
Eyes roaming brimfull
Through the rough brine of day
Almost aimless
That forgets the very ocean within
Delivering us only to the glare
Of loveless hands that do not know
What they are about
Birthings whose love possesses no question
The touch of the beastly
Creatures of this happy place
On which love yet holds sway.

The Quiet Time

when you've gone to sleep
is mine like a moon-lit glen
midst the dark forest at night
which steps lightly
all about me in dreams
adjusting our covers
in a rustling of imaginings
open to the darkling hours
that create the lives of my dreams
leaving my eyes full
of sparkling misty sight
bright in the lost minutes
of many an interrupted dream
now mine.

This Hour

This day is my glory.
This day that was tomorrow
Now is my dream become reality.
It is as if I am finally
grown tall enough
To reach that top shelf of my soul.

World

We walk through this world of governments
There is no place to escape to
We must retreat into the forests
The joy of our minds will blossom in time
Doors will open relative to the bliss we find
The love and succor we give
Perhaps will reflect a good light

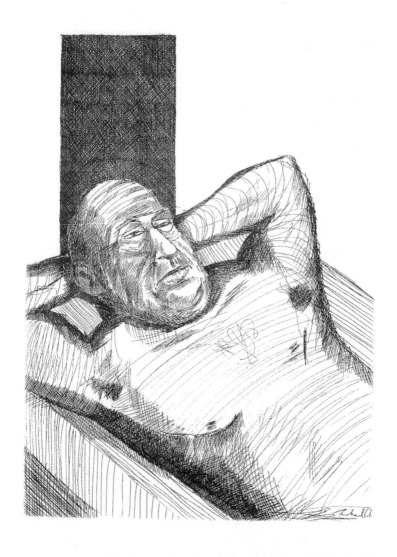

The Sweet Things In Life

I wanted once
Fortune and fame:
I was a small person
with a long way to go;
Lonely in my heart of hearts
I found the darkness that is
Powerful and true
All around me.
We walk in the shadows,
Death stalks us night and day, but
The light guides us
We emerge, finally, unscathed:
In the pure flame only
flesh ages and suffers.
Ultimately we walk with God:
The skies are full of song:
The earth blossoms beneath us;
Our arms are full of flowers.

Reclaimed

My life reclaimed.
The old clothing cast off
Tattered from struggle.
A new robe donned.
I proclaim the wonder of this world :
Honor the life within each of us ;
Rededicate myself to today......
I reach out to clasp the hand of tomorrow
In silent ceremony, graduating to a new life.

The American Continent

In the fantastic joy blossom
Of sky touching earth
Ageless mountains thrusting
Into the clouds
Rivers whose glorious flow
Rapes the terrain
With nourishing waters
Leaving a glory of growth
Topsoil full of new life
Spurting centuries
Of forests and a world of creatures
Rampant on the green landscape
Endless fields of wild corn and grain
And bison herds, killed and reborn
Caribou, like antlered angels
Roaming the northern stretches
Free and clothed in their own beauteous bounty.

Men worshipping the creatures that nourish them;
Wearing the skins, eating the flesh of their spirit
gods.
Only weary of life in the cold of the winter night

When tired bodies, tired bones float to sleep
Empty of the struggles
That unite their kind
In joyous striving to
Continue the days of their happiness
On a continent that sings to them
Of the hunt and the feasting thereafter
Of family and worship
Of nobility in life and in death.

Winter's Pause In The SunLight

This is the sacred moment
When a red pavilion bird-house hangs
Gently swinging in our cove
In the afternoon winter sun I sit bundled,
Huddled against the rising wind
In anticipation of a warm morning breeze:
Joyous at the approach of Spring !

"A Delicate Thing"

In ignorant pain
"A delicate thing" broken many times
Put back together catch as catch can
With glue from a glue pot of horses' hooves and hide
Torn asunder like these ponies, reassembled on a bet.

Bones extravagantly broken:
Mended with the spit of rain and snow.

Paint of portraits that remember the forgotten;
Words that portray lost times,
Never lived days and weeks:
A God I could sometimes not quite reach;

All these, and
An emptiness I somehow found difficult to escape.

Little Man

As we in our canoe
Pushed out on the lake
The littlest one squealed
Though in his fear
He could not tip the boat.
We returned to shore
To leave him to his own vision of safety.
Only an hour later
Returning for the second time
We found the same small boy waiting
In eager anticipation of a journey over his lake.
Richard braced his hand
And he climbed his Mt. Everest
Into our canoe.
A family now of four
Our small companion completed.
We gawked as one
At turtles large and yellow-spotted,
Egrets by the shore
And a forest of barely conceived pines
Beginning to rise from their lake
Into the fresh, stirring
Soup, primordial as we and our sky.

Only Revived by an Angel

Laundry-day was Saturday
Beyond the clotheslines out my bedroom window
There was a newsline from housewife to housewife ;
So how come no one told me
My marriage was almost over ?
About to come to a screeching halt.
I, almost to the abyss,
Everything invested
About to lose it all
In my own personal stock market crash.

The Carport Behind the Store

a moment's break...I muse :
there is no room for poetry here !
I know the pigeons are sitting on the windowsill
by my desk at home.
I cannot be there now.
there is no room for poetry here !
I must remember or anticipate a more restful time.

perhaps this is a quiet port midst the cosmic storm :
luring my words out
as the mother cat on a cold day
leads her kittens into the sun.
can we just catch the waterfall-like syllables
as they cascade to their own birthday...?
remembering I create this message for you
in a wintry carport behind a busy store
having to grasp tightly my work...
the freezing wind always trying to
pull away this page.

Near Where the Wild Cranberry Pokes its Head

Out the cedar-brown water
The one-hundred-thousand-year-old
Conches lie in pine pitch
Where the receding sea has left them.
This is a murky pool in which no one can see
Out which the white men will erect
Befouling earth and sky
Oil derricks draining the earth of her last bounty
Taking in years what only eons could accumulate,
To travel super-highways over a barren land.
But they cannot end the dominion of this maiden's
Long sought peace,
for this moment in which her proud brave
Propels her with his massive shoulders and arms
Through the boundless glory of
Their home and church ;
He has given her an ancient mother earth
As her religion
And their moment here together will exist eternally.

Haiku

Dawn on chill'd wood porch
Tiny circle within the circle
Raccoon Family Footprints !

1979 – 1997

In 1979, I went shopping for a stereo.
If I'd have known I was shopping for us...
I can still remember... I went back twice.
I went in, asked the questions I had prepared, and
listened to a few models.
They had the BSR turntable I wanted. But the receiver ?
They had a special room to listen in. I went back.
I asked my questions and listened.
I was shopping, then in 1979, for us now...

Honey, I shopped so carefully...I can remember it all now !" Did I
do good shopping ?" she asked.
They listened to the music.

" Yes. You did good shopping. Honey. Are you happy ?"" Yes. I
am. Don't you know a woman can't be happier than with tears in
her eyes. "

Success

I learn I can be a success in this life
Sing Godly tunes;
Through my art and work
Never be alone!

I want time to remember me
Know my suffering
The final joy
Of these years stretched out like pearls
On the horizon --- weeks like a thousand suns and
moons
All I know and love
That you, I pray --- the children I never had
Will remember me
And smile!

The Boat Nears the Shore

Once there was no tomorrow
Now she lies before me like a soft sweet plain.
After such a long tempestuous journey
The boat nears the shore
And with slow dignity
Glides itself toward the waiting dock

The Light Appears

The light appears on the mountains :
Joy is mine --- I only ask
The freedom to make myself
As I am wanting to be

Two Faces

You drew 2 faces on two green leaves
They were who we were
Like us
They yellowed with age
Shriveled until they crumpled
Fell "Dust to Dust" in
The Palm of His Hand
Caught in the wind of His Breath
We are all a dream
Scattered on the thoughts of the living.

I Stand in my Doorway

In memory of Amadou Dialo

In a light of old shame.
I look to and fro
For the bullets
That sent my black brother
sprawling in his vestibule.

Near

As I near
The precipice
I see more clearly
How near has become far
And far near.
Our paths like the uncountable
Earthworms
Reach to the core
Of creation
Lead us as children
Past each other
Again & again in this endless night
Until we find
The even-handed honor of earth's
Motherly embrace.

Passage

I try to make a record of our lives
On a passage into tomorrow;
We all try to live out this existence
Not exhausted of meaning.
I want to stop time
Call you back
Making today to be a great ship
Delivering her voyagers
To a place the hours cannot scar---
A land yesterday's hunger, and death
Cannot reach.
In the end we know this cannot be.
It consoles us that we are not alone in this life;
Only a great storm can sink this fleet.
We hear the cold winds of winter rise.
We hear them whistling from out these portals
Gathering strength at whim
To crush our oh so foolish, little Armada !

Arbeit Macht Frei

At least for now...
Arbeit macht frei !
But where is
Auschwitz by the Sea ?
Do you live there ?
Who would know ?
Or is it a place in the mind of this world,
Where men and women work day and night
to survive...
Only to receive pink slips
If we displease Our Great Leaders
who are vacationing half the year
on their huge ranches and estates,
and do not see the People....
For 'the workers' are nothing more
than so much
'Dust under their Feet' !

World Conscience

Troubled times !
What are the people thinking ?
Seems like the world is
brewing like a coffee pot
ready to boil over on the stove.

El Venceremos !

El Jinette, 1-2006

Better To Serve in Heaven
Than to rule in Hell.
 I would rather make my stand with the
People, Than find langour in the
dungeon-like chambers
Of our Nation's self-appointed nobility.

Mighty Heir

Sometimes I dare hope
That some creation
Within me yearns for air

I Push
To bring it into the world
But this child I cannot yet bear

Looking to myself
I see tomorrow born
Into this world as a child fair.

As in a dream
We all try to make it real:
To give our small hours some mighty heir.

Tales

Brave up to the storm
All is too soon ended
We are left with our deeds
The memory of the faces we saw
And a few fond tales

Question or Answer

What question is it?
Or which answer
Reveals itself in the wind?
Whistling past this house
Howling from out our windows
Changing to quietly falling snow?

Mary Barnet-Schiff was born in New York City in 1950 and has been writing and publishing her poetry since 1965.

She is the founder of PoetryMagazine.com on the internet which has featured most of the leading poets of the world at one time or another since 1996.

She has read her poetry to worldwide audiences and first read in public in 1967 in Greenwich Village's legendary Figaro Café.

Most recently she read at the Baggot Inn on West 3rd St. in the Village.

Mary resides in Ocean County, New Jersey with her husband Richard E. Schiff, editor of the Greenwich Village Gazette.